How To Copyr[...]
Acquire An ISBN Number

By

David Foothill

David@DavidFoothill.com

Support@iPROFICIENCY.com

TABLE OF CONTENTS

>> DISCLAIMER

The information in this book does not constitute individualized legal advice. The information is provided with the understanding that the author and publisher are not engaged in rendering legal or other professional services and expressly disclaims any liability, loss or risk incurred as a consequence, directly or indirectly, of the use and application of any of the contents of this information.

This information is not a substitute for the advice of a competent legal or other professional.

The authors have made all reasonable efforts to provide current and accurate information for the readers of this eBook. The authors will not be held liable for any unintentional errors or omissions that may be found.

When using much of this information, you may be considered as acting as your own attorney. If legal or other professional advice is required, the services of a competent professional should be sought.

By providing you with this information, the authors and publishers, its advisors, agents, representatives, and employees are not rendering any legal or otherwise professional advice or service, and no representations or warranties, express or implied, are given regarding the legal or other consequences resulting from the use of this book, including but not limited to information, content and/or forms.

The material may include information, products, or services by third parties. Third Party materials comprise of the products and opinions expressed by their owners. As such, the authors and publisher of this guide do not assume responsibility or liability for any Third Party Material or opinions.

Just a note: the information in this book pertains to U.S. Copyright registration.

>> FOREWORD

Have you created an original literary work which you now consider your "intellectual property?"

If you have created a book, you most likely believe it has value and you want to make sure that it is "protected" as your original content. You will want to enforce your rights and control how it is used.

There is automatic legal protection for your work available to you under the U.S. copyright laws.

1. What this book is written for is to help you understand what copyright is, intelligently walk you through the steps of registering your literary work with the U.S. Copyright Office and explain why it is important for you to do so within 3 months of publication in the U.S.
2. This book also helps you learn how to acquire an ISBN number if you decide that you need one.

The intent is to make the explanation as simple as possible. As such, the book is written in a style as if you were sitting down with a best friend who had the experience of copyrighting his or her own books, and they were going to help you with yours.

When you finish this book, you should know exactly how to register your book at the U.S. Copyright Office, and how to acquire an ISBN number if you decide you need one.

One very important thing: We all start reading books that we don't ever get around to finishing, so I will put this very important point right here in the Foreword.

If you are going to publish a book in the U.S., you might be making a mistake not to register it with the U.S. Copyright office within 3 months of publication. This is an important issue (explained in detail in Chapter 2) that you should address whether you finish this book or not.

Best Wishes For Your Success,

David Foothill

>> Chapter 1 - IS YOUR BOOK AUTOMATICALLY COPYRIGHTED?

Let's talk about your book. You're sure it will be a best seller, a mega-hit, and you can hardly wait to publish it. You are metaphorically, if not literally "dancing in the end zone."

The natural and correct instinct is to want to protect your valuable work and you start thinking about your copyright protections because you have concerns that someone might want to use the intellectual property you created and own without your permission,

There is good news for authors, and a fact that may surprise a number of people because there is a lot of misinformation due to some major changes in the laws over the years.

Your literary work is protected by federal copyright law the minute you create it in tangible of fixed form.

1) It is "unregistered" intellectual property at this point, but it is still copyrighted right then and there. (Unregistered means it has not yet been filed with the U.S. Copyright office.)
2) It may be "unpublished" intellectual property at this point, but it is still copyrighted right then and there.
3) You may or may not have affixed the Copyright Notice to the material, but it is still copyrighted right then and there.

Yes, you read that right. If you have created original work that is eligible for copyright protection, it is copyrighted, period. It is entitled to the benefits of copyright protection the second it comes out of the printer, or saved on your digital device, etc.:

- Even if you have not yet published your literary work,
- Even if you have not yet affixed the copyright notice, and
- Even if you have not yet registered it with the U.S. Copyright office.

People are sometimes confused about this because it used to be that you had to include the copyright notice (see below) on your work. That is no longer true and has not been true since March 1st, 1989.

Copyright is a form of legal protection provided by U.S. law (title 17, U. S. Code) afforded to the authors of "original works of authorship." This protection is available to both published and unpublished works, and to registered and unregistered works.

The general protection you have is

1) The right to gain financially and
2) The right to control how your work is used.

Of course, having the right to gain financially doesn't mean you will do so. Further, posting your content somewhere, like a web page, doesn't give someone else the right to use it as in re-posting it.

Note here before we continue that not everything you create is copyrighted.

For instance, an idea in your head is not copyrighted and generally, neither is a name, title, slogan, logo, fact, procedure, process, system, method of operation, concept, principle, or discovery. (These may be protected under a different set of laws such as a patent or a trademark.)

TRADEMARKS

You may have noticed above that names and titles cannot be copyrighted. That doesn't mean that one hasn't been trademarked.

This is a little off the Copyright point, but the United States Trademark and Patent Office can be very useful to you in regard to who owns what.

You can visit their website at http://www.uspto.gov/trademarks/index.jsp and type in some of your key terms to conduct a "Trademark Search" to see if someone does actually own the right to a name, etc.

BEST PRACTICES

You may be asking yourself; if my book is already copyrighted can I just stop reading right here?

You could of course, but I don't recommend it. In business, every industry has what is known as a set of "best practices."

What "best practices" are is a method, or series of steps, that the leading organizations use because they have been time-tested and field-proven and lead to success. Here are a series of steps generally considered to be the "best practices" regarding your book's copyright protections.

1) Use a copyright notice."
2) Register your book with U.S. Copyright office within 3 months of U.S. publication to maximize your legal rights and also satisfy the "U.S. mandatory deposit requirements.
3) Acquire an ISBN Number if you are going to do anything other than publish your book as an e-book.

We are going to cover all three best practices and two additional ones that are recommended.

COPYRIGHT NOTICE

The Copyright Notice is no longer required for your content to be copyrighted, but it is still something that you absolutely should do.

There are typically three parts to the copyright notice

1) The word "Copyright" and the copyright symbol ©.
2) The year it is first published in the U.S., and
3) The copyright holder or owner of the rights.

Here is a 4th option .After your copyright notice, include: "All Rights Reserved." This offers extra notice that you demand all rights offered under the U.S. Copyright laws.

A 5th option is text that spells out what people may not do. For example:

No part of this publication shall be reproduced, transmitted or resold in whole or in part in any form, without the prior written consent of the authors. All trademarks and registered trademarks appearing are the property of their respective owners.

Here is an example from the front of this book:

Copyright © 2012, iPROFICIENCY All Rights Reserved

No part of this publication shall be reproduced, transmitted or resold in whole or in part in any form, without the prior written consent of the authors. All trademarks and registered trademarks appearing are the property of their respective owners.

I repeat for clarification: You should include these notifications at the front of your literary work as a solid business practice. It is not required, however, for your work to be copyrighted in the U.S.

A question that is frequently asked is "can I use the copyright notice before I register my book with the U.S. Copyright office?" The answer is yes, and the reason is your book was copyrighted the second it came into existence, whether you registered it with the U.S. Copyright office or not.

One last point is that there is some international cooperation in regard to copyrights and you are best positioned in the most countries by affixing the copyright notice.

LENGTH OF COPYRIGHT

Since January 1, 1978, your literary work copyright protection will last for your life, plus 70 years. For an anonymous work, a pseudonymous work, or a work made for hire, the copyright endures for a term of 95 years from the year of its first publication or a term of 120 years from the year of its creation, whichever expires first.

>> Chapter 2 - REGISTRATION WITH THE U.S. COPYRIGHT OFFICE: THE 3 MONTH TICKING CLOCK

There are significant and crucial business and legal reasons to register your work with the U.S. Copyright office.

The chances you are going to have to sue somebody are very slim, but why not protect yourself to the highest degree possible? (Also, there is a "mandatory deposit requirement we will talk about in a minute and registering your e-book will satisfy that requirement as well.)

Establishing a public record of your work and when it was created by registering your work with the U.S. Copyright office within 3 months of publication gives you legal remedies and awards you may not be entitled to otherwise, *such as forfeiting the right to sue for statutory damages and attorney fees.*

Let's suppose that you find that someone else is distributing copies of your work freely or for profit. That they have blatantly taken the text from your book, changed the cover and the title, and are now publishing it as their book.

The only remedy for such a violation has to be initiated by you; most likely with the assistance of an attorney.

Here is the startling fact that people often find out too late: If you didn't register your work within three months of publication you have generally forfeited your right to statutory damages and attorney fees.

What are statutory damages and why are they a big deal?

Statutory damages are set dollar amounts in civil law where the amount that has to be paid is based on a statute (a written part of a law) rather than the actual damage that occurred. In the real world this is critical for you to be able to enforce your rights as explained below.

A person who infringes on another person's copyright can be liable for statutory damages up to $30,000.00 for each work infringed on, and in the case of willful infringement, that amount could be increased up to $150,000.00, plus attorney fees.

But, as was stated above, if you didn't register your work within three months of publication with the U.S. Copyright office, you have generally forfeited your right to statutory damages and attorney fees.

If you can't sue for statutory damages and attorney fees, what can you sue for?

The short answer is you can sue for "damages," such as the loss you have incurred because of the other parties copyright infringement.

Good luck with that because in most cases it can be very hard to prove what you would have made, or have lost, because someone violated your copyright.

Yes, you might be able to prove large losses, for example, where one movie studio is suing another movie studio, but what are the damages for someone ripping off parts of your e-book?

Unless you can sue for statutory damages and attorney fees, violators aren't going to exactly be shaking in their boots over your cease and desist letter; and unless you have registered your work with the U.S. Copyright office within three months of publication in the U.S., in most cases you cannot sue for statutory damages and attorney fees.

Do you see the issue here?

Your enforcement efforts are going to have very little "teeth" if you can only sue for your losses and damages and you can't also threaten to sue for statutory damages and attorney fees.

But if the violator receives a letter advising them that they are illegally using your content and you are reserving the right to sue them for big statutory damages and any attorney fees; they might pay better attention.

Do this right - - Put a copyright notice on your work and register it with the U.S. Copyright office within 3 months of "publication" for maximum legal protection. If you didn't do it then, do it now, it only costs $35.00 if you register online.

>> Chapter 3 - HAVE YOU "INFRINGED" ON ANOTHER PARTY'S COPYRIGHT?

When you submit your work to the U.S. Copyright Office, virtually all of what you submit is going to be public record and it is going to be "permanent." There is no going back to edit or change what you submitted later. So before you rush to www.copyright.gov and register your book, let's ask a few questions.

QUESTION #1

Have you infringed on anybody else's copyright content in any way?

Be honest here. I'm not sure if anybody can really claim an original idea, but are there entire paragraphs lifted out of something that has been copyrighted by somebody else?

COPYRIGHT INFRINGEMENT – THERE ARE NO COPYRIGHT POLICE

Generally speaking, there is copyright infringement if you have included content in your book that someone else owns the rights to (it is copyrighted).

Here is what people sometimes wonder at this point: "well, there are a few parts that I researched somewhere else and then I did apply my own thinking to it and changed the order of words, added a few words, etc. Is that going to fly?"

Here is a practical but non-legal answer.

Is the person or organization that owns the copyright going to think that your work is stolen from their work and sue you?

Note; the only person or organization that can sue you for copyright infringement are the parties who believe their own copyrighted content that has been infringed upon. There are no copyright police as far as I know, but there may be somebody who considers themselves an unhappy victim (and that was when the trouble started).

"You" may not think a person or organization could successfully sue you, but that is not always the right issue to focus on.

What you should also consider is "does the other party think they could prevail?" I say that because litigation is expensive.

Lawsuits are settled out of court all the time. Why? They are settled out of court because it can be less expensive to settle than to fight.

So I'll ask again. Is there somebody that is going to take offense at your creation because they believe that it is really their creation, and who will sue you because they think it is intellectual property that they own?

You don't want it to be a close enough call that your attorney will be advising you to write a settlement check rather than fight it out in court

If it should go to court and you are found guilty of infringing on someone's copyright, you may be liable for statutory damages up to $30,000.00 for each work infringed, and in the case of willful infringement that amount could be increased up to $150,000.00, plus attorney fees.

Right now, before you submit your work to the copyright office is the time to ask yourself if there is anything to be worried or concerned about.

If the answer is "no, great, but let's take one more look before we proceed to the next question.

Just to be clear, you now understand it doesn't matter what the original creator of the content did or didn't do. If they created it, they own it, and it is copyrighted.

About the only exceptions are "fair use" and "public domain" which are explained later in this book.

QUESTION #2 - WORK FOR HIRE

This could be a long chapter, but if you wrote a book you have enough common sense to answer this question.

Is somebody going to claim work for hire violations?

You may be bound in several ways by an "employment agreement" that sets forth many areas and provisions between you and your employer.

Under a "work for hire" arrangement, the employer becomes the owner and owns the right to register the work with the U.S. Copyright office.

>> Chapter 4 - WHO IS THE AUTHOR, THE CLAIMANT, AND THE CORRESPONDENT?

You have written a masterpiece; congratulations!

Does that automatically make you the owner?

What rights do you have as the owner?

Can you transfer some of those rights to another party?

Who owns the rights if there are co-authors?

Many of these questions (rights) are established via the U.S. Copyright office registration process.

AUTHOR

First there is a place on the U.S. Government Copyright Registration form for the applicant (to make this easy we will make the applicant you) to designate the author(s). You can put your name in the author field. There is also the option to make it pseudonymous and write in a pseudonym commonly referred to as a pen name (discussed later).

CLAIMANT

There will also be a place on the registration form to designate the claimant. The claimant is also the "Owner of the copyright rights."

You, as the author will always be the original claimant who is the owner of the copyright and the rights that go along with that.

However, you can legally transfer your rights, say to a publisher, and if it is the publisher that now owns the rights and is completing the U.S. Copyright registration application, then they would list themselves as the claimant. That means they would be stating that they own the rights and protections attached to the intellectual property afforded by copyright law.

RIGHTS AND PERMISSIONS

There is a place for you to designate who should be contacted regarding the use of your work (rights and permissions).

For example, if some big Hollywood movie studio wants to contact someone about film rights; who should they contact?

Various answers put on the registration application could be you, your business agent, your publisher, your neighbor who is a business whiz; the applicant will decide who should go in this section of the registration application.

CORRESPONDENT

The U.S. Copyright office will also want to know who should be contacted if there is an issue with the registration process, such as incomplete information.

>> Chapter 5 - WHAT ARE THE DISTINCTIONS BETWEEN COPYRIGHT, REGISTRATION & MANDATORY DEPOSIT?

It is easy to get a bit confused at first concerning the difference between copyright, registration of your work with the U.S. Copyright Office, and mandatory deposit.

COPYRIGHT

We noted earlier that your work is copyrighted upon creation; it enjoys protection under the federal copyright laws immediately.

REGISTRATION

There are business and legal reasons why you will want to "register" your work with the U.S. Copyright Office within 3 months of it being published. .The primary reason is to establish your right to statutory damages if you should have to sue someone, but there are several other solid business reasons as well.

MANDATORY DEPOSIT

There is also a U.S. requirement (17 U.S.C. section 407) that requires you (or the owner if you have transferred ownership of your work) to "deposit" two completed copies of your work to the U.S. Library Of Congress. This must be done within 3 months after a work is published and is referred to as "Mandatory Deposit."

You are reading this correctly. If you literary work is published in the U.S., there is a legal requirement for the owner of the Copyright to deposit within 3 months of publication, the required number of copies (2) with the U.S. Copyright Office. (Note: This requirement is waived for an e-book.)

TWO BIRDS WITH ONE STONE

If you "register" your work with the U.S. Copyright Office, that will satisfy the "Mandatory Deposit" requirement.

The only advantage I can think of by completing the "Mandatory Deposit" requirement and not "registering" your work is the registration fee (only $35.00 if you do it online).

O.K., let's review:

1) Your book is copyrighted the moment it comes into existence.
2) You should register it with the U.S. Copyright office within 3 months of it being "published in the U.S." for maximum legal protection.
3) When you register the book with the U.S. Copyright office, the registration also satisfies the mandatory deposit requirement.

If for some reason, you don't want to register your work, but you do want to satisfy the mandatory deposit requirement, here is the address to send your two copies to:

Library of Congress
Copyright Office
Attn: 407 Deposits
101 Independence Avenue, SE
Washington, DC 20559

"ONLINE ONLY" EXEMPTION

There is an exemption for online only works. This means, for example, if you are publishing an e-book that is only going to be available online, the mandatory deposit requirement is waived.

Our recommendation, even if you are just publishing an online e-book, is to register your book within 3 months of publication in the U.S. in order to maximize your legal rights. Why take chances of any kind for $35.00?

FOREIGN WORKS

Once a foreign work becomes published in the U.S., it also becomes subject to all U.S. mandatory deposit requirements.

>> Chapter 6 - HOW DOES A PERSON PUBLISH UNDER A PEN NAME (PSEUDONYM) AND / OR REMAIN ANONYMOUS?

Are you going to use your real name or a pen name?

What we will cover in this book is how to register with a pseudonym if you choose to do so, and what impact that is going to have on the registration page process.

When you register your work with the U.S. Copyright office and you come to the "author" field; the author does not have to be identified by his or her real name.

If you want to use a pen name you leave the author fields empty and you check off the "pseudonymous" box and write in the pen name (pseudonym) in the space provided.

When this happens, your work becomes pseudonymous.

Note, an author's name is a database field that is online searchable at the www.copyright.gov website.

So as stated, if you don't want your real name to be listed as the author, don't complete the fields that ask for the author's name. You would leave those database fields blank on the registration form and check off the "pseudonymous" box and write in the pen name (pseudonym).

You may be asking yourself how is the U.S. Copyright office going to know that you are the person who owns the copyright?

They will know because of the information completed in the "claimant' section of the application.

This process should suffice for people that want to write under a pen name rather than their real name.

However, just so you know, registering your copyright with a pseudonym is not going to shield your real name from someone who wants to look just a bit more deeply than the book cover.

Someone could still easily find your name during an online search by searching the title and seeing that you are the claimant, and put two and two together and come to the conclusion that you, as the claimant, are also the author using a pen name.

"Who is the claimant" is a field that is returned when someone does an online search at www.copyright.gov.

There are people that want to go a step further than just write under a pen name. The reason they want to write under a pen name is because they want to be completely anonymous. They want to remain 100% private.

If this is really your goal:

1) You should get some professional assistance either by contacting an attorney, or
2) You could use a publisher who would maintain your privacy, or
3) You could set up your own publishing company (although most company registrations are also public and searchable online).

If you complete your application with both your real name as the author and also use a pen name, your book will have the normal copyright protection, which would be your lifetime, plus 75 years.

If you leave the author field blank and only enter the pen name, the copyright protection will be shorter of 95 years from the publication date or 120 years from the creation date.

Disclaimer here: Just a reminder that the author is not an attorney and this is not legal advice, nor is any of the other information in this book to be relied on as legal advice.

>> Chapter 7 - WHAT SEARCHABLE INFORMATION FROM YOUR REGISTRATION IS OPEN TO THE PUBLIC?

For various reasons you may want to know what information in your registration application at the U.S. Copyright office is going to be viewable to the public.

In Chapter 1 we discussed that when you submit your copyright to the Library of Congress, much of what you submit is going to be public record, and it is going to be permanent.

Let's start with your e-mail address which you need to provide when establishing an account to log in to the system. That e-mail address you use to register with the U.S. Copyright office is not searchable online or available on the public record.

ONLINE SEARCH RESULTS

Here are the fields that are included in the result of an online search at the U.S. Copyright office website:

Type of Work:
Registration Number / Date:
Application Title:
Title:
Description:
Copyright Claimant:
Date of Creation:
Authorship on Application:
Copyright Note:
Names:

It would help to do a search yourself of one of your favorite authors. I did one with the name of a famous mystery writer and found 284 registrations.

SEARCHING PHYSICAL RECORDS AT THE U.S. COPYRIGHT OFFICE

A person can also conduct an in-person search of copyright registrations at the U.S. Copyright offices. The difference from an online search is almost all of the information on your registration application is available through a search at the U.S. Copyright office, and the information can be copied using copy machines provided in the U.S. copyright office.

For a fee, you can have the U.S. Copyright personnel perform various types of searches for you as well.

>> Chapter 8 - SHOULD YOU SELF-PUBLISH YOUR BOOK?

I have heard that it worked out well for certain authors to let someone else publish their book and handle all the related activities.

That was then, however, and this is now, and if you are reading this book, you have probably already made the decision to self-publish your book.

Or maybe you just don't want to let your work out of your hands until you have safely registered it with the U.S. government.

Here is the point, however, of including this chapter in this book. Whether you are or are not going to publish your book yourself, I still think it is a good idea to register your book with the U.S. Copyright office as soon as it is finished. I believe the $35.00 will provide you great "peace of mind."

You don't want it to ever be said that you missed the 3 month window between the first U.S. Publishing and the registration with the U.S. Copyright office.

Does he mean publication ?

>> Chapter 9 - TRANSFER STATEMENTS

Do transfer statements really deserve their own chapter?

I think they do because they are confusing to anyone not familiar with the process, and clarity will be helpful to those individuals.

We don't want anyone getting "stuck" at the registration step because they are confused about something.

When the U.S. Copyright registration application is being completed, an important part of the process is establishing the claimant, because the claimant owns all the rights afforded by copyright law.

If the claimant is also the author, that is pretty clear and simple.

If someone other than the author is saying they are the claimant, they need to certify on the registration form that they have the legal right to do so, and they must affirm that the "transfer of rights" from the author to them has been done lawfully (for the most part in writing).

The registration process goes so far as to require a declaration of how the transfer was made. In other words, they must declare how the transfer of copyright ownership rights was "transferred" from one party to another.

For example, a publisher and an author would normally have a written agreement that would transfer the ownership rights from the author to the publisher.

There are five options for declaration:

1) By written agreement(s) with author(s) named on the application / certificate
2) By written agreement(s) with individual contributors not named on the application / certificate
3) By written agreement(s) with authors named and contributors not named on the application/certificate
4) By written agreement
5) Other (There is a box to provide any clarification needed when choosing this option)

The actual transfer agreement is not submitted as part of the registration process; but the applicant is certifying to the U.S. Government, that the transfer agreements exists and is signed by the appropriate parties.

Don't make the mistake of thinking you will complete a transfer statement later and check off that it exists if it does not. Do it right and if you are going to transfer rights, have the transfer agreement finalized and signed prior to registering your book with the U.S. Copyright office.

Remember the clock starts ticking once you publish your book, so be sure to allow yourself adequate time to complete this step before the important "3 months from publication in the U.S." runs out.

There is more information available from the U.S. Copyright website at http://www.copyright.gov/eco/help-claimant.html.

>> Chapter 10 - WHAT RIGHTS COME WITH A COPYRIGHT?

Generally speaking, your rights to the work you own the copyright to include:

- The right to reproduce (copy) the work,
- The right to make derivative works of the original,
- The right to distribute copies, and
- The right to perform / display the work publicly.

These are the rights of the copyright owner, and only the owner, of the copyright unless they are transferred to another party.

The most obvious example would be to transfer copyright rights from an author to a publisher via a contract.

Although rights may be transferred, the transfer is generally not valid unless that transfer is in writing and signed by the owner of the rights conveyed or the owner's duly authorized agent.

The most important point about your rights is that they are "exclusive" to you (or any party you have transferred rights to).

The burden of enforcing your rights are also up to you (or any party you have transferred rights to). If you want to maintain your rights to copyright protection to the maximum degree, then a good start is to follow the "best practices" outlined in Chapter 1 and / or seek the advice of legal counsel.

>> Chapter 11 - WHAT IS FAIR USE?

Fair use means that under certain conditions and circumstances:

- Someone else may be allowed to use part of your copyrighted work, or
- You may use part of a copyrighted work you don't own.

Examples of fair use might include:

- Someone would use part of your book in commentary to post a review
- Part of it may appear in a snippet in a search engine result
- Someone might want to use part of it for news reporting
- Someone might want to use part of it for research
- Someone might want to use part of it for teaching
- Someone might want to use part of it for library archiving

Remember, there are no copyright police but my recommendation here is to be cautious, and even better, use an attorney experienced in this area if you have any concerns.

What is or is not fair use is really a matter for legal experts.

Here is the link to what the U.S. Copyright Office has to say on "Fair Use:" http://www.copyright.gov/fls/fl102.html

>> Chapter 12 - WHAT ARE DERIVATIVE WORKS?

In the United States, the Copyright Act defines "derivative work" in 17 U.S.C. § 101 as a work based upon a pre-existing work in which a work may be recast, transformed, or adapted. A work consisting of editorial revisions, annotations, elaborations, or other modifications which, as a whole, represent an original work of authorship, is a "derivative work".

Suffice it to say that the very tricky part here is knowing when a work crosses over a line from "original work" that now makes it a "derivative work."

Since we didn't want to create a 300-page book we will fall back on "the scope of this book was to help you understand the principles and practices of copyrighting your book" and to let you know there is a legal concept known as derivative work.

The best advice here is the advice provided in the previous chapter: use an attorney experienced in this area if you have any concerns.

Here is the link to more information on derivative works from the U.S. Copyright website http://www.copyright.gov/circs/circ14.pdf.

>> Chapter 13 - WHAT IS PUBLIC DOMAIN?

For the most part, public domain refers to intellectual property that has never been copyrighted, or the copyright has expired. The example everyone uses is the work of Shakespeare.

If I wanted to "Cut and Paste" one of Shakespeare's plays right into the middle of this chapter, I could legally do so because the copyright has expired and it is now considered to be in the public domain.

This means you can consider what is in the Public Domain as fair game; but as always, exercise caution.

The example given in every copyright lecture is "Snow White And The Seven Dwarfs."

The copyright protection of the original content has expired, but adaptations of the work are copyrighted by people that may have no sense of humor about their rights being infringed upon.

Get some legal help if there is any question, or just to be sure.

You may think something is in the public domain, but that doesn't mean it necessarily is.

BONUS: Are you familiar with "Project Gutenberg and their interest in "fair use?"

Project Gutenberg offers over 40,000 free e-books and over 100,000 free e-books are available through their other Resources. You can check it out at http://www.gutenberg.org.

>> Chapter 14 - HOW TO REGISTER YOUR WORK ONLINE AT THE U.S. COPYRIGHT OFFICE'S WEBSITE

Finally; it took us to chapter 14 to get to the steps to register your book with the U.S. Copyright office, but I hope you found the process worth it.

The steps below explain how to register your e-book online using the "eCO" (Electronic Copyright Office). You don't have to file online, but as they say on ESPN "C'mon Man," you wrote a book and bought an e-book, you should be able to do this online.

There is also a savings for registering your work online. If you register online, the fee will be U.S. $35.00. If you print out the forms and mail them in the fee is $65.00.

This is also a good place to talk about one of the most important roles of the U.S. Copyright office - to be a central place of record where copyright registrations are collected and stored. This is not insignificant in importance, and while they perform many other valuable functions, professionally gathering the information from your registration and keeping it safe is critical to you and to our entire system of copyright protection.

Step 1 - Go To the U.S. Copyright Office website at www.copyright.gov.

Step 2 - Click on the icon that says "How To Register Your Work."

Step 3 - Read the security warnings and continue.

Step 4 - Click on the icon that says "eCO Tutorial (PowerPoint)" and watch the PowerPoint http://www.copyright.gov/eco/eco-tutorial.pps. You can also download a PDF copy at http://www.copyright.gov/eco/eco-tutorial.pdf.

You may be asking why you had to buy this book to recommend that you watch a PowerPoint on a government website. Here are the reasons:

- The Government's PowerPoint is outstanding; a well done piece of communication (apparently not all branches of our government are dysfunctional and hats are off to the U.S. Government personnel).

- The PowerPoint shows you the actual screens with animation - a superior way to convey the information
- If you prefer a printed explanation, you can save the PDF on your computer, and print it out (once again you have the actual screens with most of the animated captions).
- Remember our dual goals 1) To help walk you through the steps of copyrighting your e-book and acquiring an ISBN number and 2) To accomplish this in as easy and efficient a manner as possible. Watching the Government's PowerPoint is the best way to understand the registration application.

Step 5 - Either log-in to the www.copyright.gov website if you are a registered user. If you are not, you should register.

Click on the icon that says "Start Registration"

Step 6 - Once you are registered and begin the registration process, there is a checklist of sorts down the left column. As you complete each item the website will track your progress.

Step 7 - From the drop down menu choose "literary work" and continue.

Step 8 - Add the title of your book and save, and then continue. If you are just registering one book, you do not need to be concerned about volume, number, or issue date. (The Title Type is "Title of work being registered")

Step 9 - Check off whether your e-book has been published or not (there is a guideline on the form to help you answer this question.

Complete the year of completion

Step 9 - Check off whether there has been a pre-registration of the work and fill in the requested information if this applies.

Step 10 - The author: If you are the author and also the person who is registered at the www.copyright.gov website, click the "add me" icon. If you are not the author or going to be using a pseudonym, click the "New" icon to add the name of the author.

Step 11 - fill in the information for the author; either as an individual or as an organization, but not both.

If you are using a pseudonym, check off the pseudonym box and write in the pseudonym in box for that information. Save and continue.

Step 12 - Check off whether you are a U.S. Citizen or your country of domicile, but not both. This is a required field.

Step 13 - Where it asks for the author's contribution, check the "Text" box and the editing box. If the author also contributed original graphics, check off the appropriate boxes as well.

Step 14 - If there are multiple authors, keep adding them by clicking the "new" icon until you are finished adding authors.

Step 15 - The claimant: If you wrote and are copyrighting the book, you are the claimant and click the "add me" icon. If someone else is going to own the copyright (publisher, employer), you should check the "New" icon and add the information.

Step 16 - Complete the Claimant information.

Step 17 - Limitation Of Claim: does the work you are copyrighting include any preexisting material? If so, complete the fields on the form.

Step 18: Rights & Permissions: Who is the right person or organization to contact regarding your copyrighted content?

Step 19: Correspondent: This is the person the U.S. Copyright office will contact if there are any questions or issues regarding the copyright application.

Step 20: Mail Certificate: This is the contact that will receive the registration certificate when finalized.

Step 21: Special Handling is available if circumstances necessitate it.

Step 22: Certify that you are legally authorized to be requesting the copyright.

Step 23: Start your own numbering system of your works.

Step 24 - Save your template because that way you won't have to complete much of the information when you come back with your next work. Also, don't forget to save your work as you go along in case you lose your Internet connection midstream etc.

Step 25 - If you are copyrighting multiple works click on "add more services." Otherwise proceed to "checkout."

Step 26 - If you don't have a "deposit account" click on the "Credit Card / ACH" icon.

Step 27 - You can pay by electronic funds transfer or credit card. Choose one and complete the information and click the "Submit Payment" icon (a receipt e-mail will be sent to you).

Step 28 - You're not done, you need to submit a copy of your work to the copyright office. Since you are copyrighting an e-book, you should be able to pull this off electronically. "Click the "upload digital copies" icon.

Step 29 - Select the files from your computer to upload, fill in the names of the files, and click on the "Submit Files To Copyright Office" icon.

Step 30 - Viola!! (If you have the Upload Successful screen showing). You will get an e-mail confirming that your content has successfully been uploaded to the copyright office.

Step 31 - You can check the status of your submission at any time by returning to the www.copyright.gov website, logging in, and finding the "Check Case Status" tab in the left column and then clicking on the "My Applications" icon.

Step 32 - There is even a way for you to call or e-mail the copyright office:

For Technical issues contact: Copyright Technology Office, 202-707-3002 or e-mail to ctoinfo@loc.gov. For Registration issues contact: Copyright Public Information Office, 202-707-3000 or e-mail to copyinfo@loc.gov.

As previously mentioned, your content has always been copyrighted, but these steps now register your content with the U.S. Copyright Office, and they also satisfy the mandatory deposit requirement. Congratulations, and chill the bubbly for when your certificate arrives in 2 - 3 months.

>> Chapter 15 - WHAT ARE ISBN NUMBERS AND HOW IS ONE ACQUIRED?

Here is an extremely brief history of ISBN numbers. ISBN stands for International Standard Book Number. They started in Dublin, Ireland in 1965 as 9 digit numbers and evolved to 2007 when they became 10 and 13 digit numbers which they still are today.

An ISBN number identifies a title's binding, edition, and the publisher.

The issuance of an ISBN number is country specific, so the process is different in Canada, for instance, than in the U.S.

In the United States, a privately held company R. R. Bowker (http://www.bowker.com/en-US/) is the responsible entity that issues ISBN numbers.

If you are publishing a physical book, you need to have a barcode that reveals your ISBN number so people and organizations that distribute, sell and purchase books (bookstores, libraries, retail stores, etc.) have an easy way to identify the book itself, and also to look up the pricing for the book.

ISBN Numbers are not free (no surprise) and the charge varies depending upon the number of ISBNs purchased, with prices ranging from $125.00 for a single number, and less when purchased in larger numbers. For instance if you buy a package of 10 the cost is reduced to $250.00, or $25.00 each, and at 1,000, the cost is $1,000.00 or only $1.00 each. (That may be the world record for quantity discounts.)

Also, you need a separate ISBN number for each version of your book (paperback, hardback, etc.). This is mainly true because there may be a different pricing level for each work (paperback vs. hardback), but there are also other identity label reasons as well.

The question you have to ask yourself is do you really need an ISBN number? The short answer is "yes" if you expect to publish a printed copy that will be sold in bookstores, available in libraries, etc. You need to invest in an ISBN number because most bookstores are not going to carry a book without an ISBN number and a Bookland EAN Barcode.

Oh, did I forget to mention? The Bookland EAN Barcode is separate and costs an additional flat fee of $25.00 (per version of your book).

Look, it takes money to make money, but there are a few inexpensive, but not necessarily complete, solutions to explore.

If you are only going to be distributing your book at the start as an e-book through the major online sellers that don't require an ISBN number, and not begin with a printed version, you can delay your investment in an ISBN number if you want. You do not need an ISBN number to sell an online version of your book through the Amazon KDP program for example.

If you are working through a publisher, they will acquire the ISBN and EAN Barcode for you (They probably purchased their stock at the $1.00 each rate).

The Amazon owned "Create Space" service has discounted and even free options available; but your distribution will be limited to their list, which does not open up your book to the entire universe of book sellers. Still, this is not a bad option for a first-time author.

I do recommend you visit the R. R. Bowker (http://www.bowker.com/en-US/) website whether you are going to purchase an ISBN Number right now or not. They offer many services for authors and publishers that could be of value.

> > CHAPTER 16 - THE DIGITAL MILLENNIUM COPYRIGHT ACT (DMCA) / DIGITAL RIGHTS MANAGEMENT (DRM)

While this book is designed to help a person understand the issues surrounding the copyright of their book and acquiring an ISBN Number, readers should also have knowledge of the Digital Millennium Copyright Act.

The reason is that the Internet and digital books are now such a big part of the book business, DRM is sure to come up whenever the issue of copyrights is being discussed.

The Digital Millennium Copyright Act (DMCA) was passed in law and signed by President Clinton in 1998.

Like any law it is complex, and this review won't do it justice except to provide you with "awareness."

The simple way to look at this is to ask yourself "who owns the digital rights?"

Put in terms of books, for instance, if you pay for a physical book at a bookstore, "do you own that copy?"

Of course you own the book you purchased. You can take it with you as you travel, you can loan it to a friend, and you can re-sell it (although even re-selling a book that has been purchased has been known to have been legally challenged).

In the case of the physical book there is implied ownership even though the content it is protected by copyright so that, for instance, you can't redistribute the content even though you own the physical book.

Now, if you pay for an e-book and download it to your computer, "do you own that copy?"

That question falls under the scope of "The Digital Millennium Copyright Act." and would require another lengthy book to properly answer.

But, let's look at some of the issues.

If you pay for your e-book and download it to your computer, may you legally:

- Transfer it to another device?
- Make a copy and give it to a friend?
- Sell it to someone else?
- Have it removed from your device by the party that sold it to you if you violate their "Terms Of Service?"
- Demand privacy over how the content was viewed, how frequently it was accessed, what notes were made, etc.?

An example, of Digital Rights Management (DRM) would be a case where you have purchased something to be used on one device (let's say an e-reader) but would not be able to transfer it to another device (let's say a smart-phone or your laptop computer).

If you don't already know this, DRM is very controversial, and there are many groups that say it threatens the very core of our freedom. Whichever side you come down on, this is sure to be a burning issue going forward.

DMCA TAKEDOWN NOTICE

Here is one more issue of this area to look at from a very high altitude. Someone might knowingly or unknowingly put copyrighted content on the Internet. Either way, the owner of the copyright can request that the content be removed.

The controversy here is who is held liable for copyright infringement if it has occurred. Is it just the offender, or is the ISP (Internet Service Provider) or the Aggregator (think YouTube) also liable?

The Internet Service Providers and Aggregators aren't going to wait to see if they are or not liable. If they receive a takedown notice that complies with the DMCA laws and procedures, they are generally going to remove the content first and ask questions later.

You can imagine how controversial this has become and to add fuel to the fire, there are many reported instances of people and organizations that are abusing this by filing nuisance lawsuits, false claims against competitor's websites, etc.

You can stay tuned to this issue by visiting our website at: http://www.HowToCopyrightBooks.com.

>> CHAPTER 17 - U.S. COPYRIGHT OFFICE REFERENCE SOURCES

There is a plethora of information available at the U.S. Copyright Office website. Here are the links the author believes are the most valuable:

U.S. Copyright Website: www.copyright.gov .

Publications On Copyright - The website with direct links to all the forms and publications at: http://www.copyright.gov/circs/.

Copyright Basics - http://www.copyright.gov/circs/circ1.pdf.

Frequently Asked Questions about Copyright - http://www.copyright.gov/help/faq/.

Search Copyright Information - http://www.copyright.gov/records/.

Mailing Address: Library of Congress
Copyright Office- COPUBS
101 Independence Avenue SE
Washington, DC 20559

Forms And Publications Hotline: If you know which application forms and circulars you want, request them 24 hours a day from the Forms and Publications Hotline at (202) 707-9100. Leave a recorded message.

Registration with Paper Forms: Paper versions of all forms are available on the Copyright Office website; and staff will send them to you by postal mail upon request. Call the Public Information Office at (202) 707-3000 or 1-877-476-0778 or the Forms and Publications Hotline at (202) 707-9100.

>> EPILOGUE

Thanks for investing in this book and taking the time to read this far. I sincerely hope you found it of value.

The most important thing from my perspective is that you have found this book helpful to your own success

Can you take a minute and rate this book and / or offer a comment on the site from which you purchased it if we have met or exceeded your expectations and been of help?

It would be greatly appreciated by me and may also be useful to someone else who was in your shoes before you purchased this book.

Here is what I promised:

1. That you will save yourself several hours of research and quickly and easily learn about the "best practices" of book copyrights.
2. In less than 60 minutes you will understand your copyright protections, how to register your book with the U.S. Copyright office, satisfy the "mandatory deposit" requirement, and also acquire an ISBN number if you decide one is needed.
3. This book will spell out exactly what you need to do, where to do it, and how to do it.

If I succeeded I would be grateful for your recommendation.

If you would like to stay updated on significant changes in the area of copyrights, please visit the iPROFICIENCY website at: www.howtocopyrightbooks.com.

Best Wishes For Your Success,

David Foothill

Made in the USA
Lexington, KY
09 May 2014